History of America

EXPLORING THE GREAT LAKES

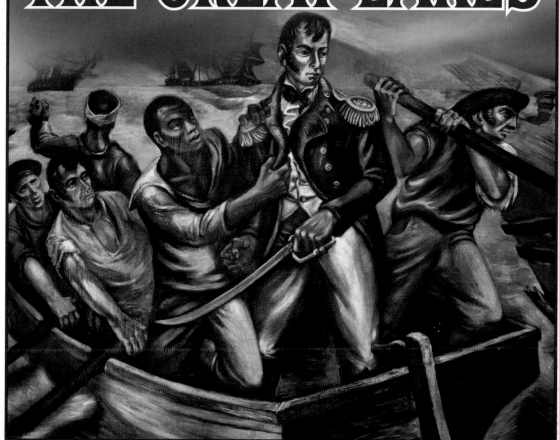

Written by **Linda Thompson**

Rourke
Educational Media

rourkeeducationalmedia.com

Scan for Related Titles
and Teacher Resources

www.rourkeeducationalmedia.com

PHOTO CREDITS: Courtesy U.S. Army, Center of Military History: pages 36, 41; Courtesy Library of Congress, Edward S. Curtis Collection: page 17; Courtesy Library of Congress, Prints and Photographs Division: pages 7, 8, 10, 12, 19, 20, 21, 25, 26, 27, 28, 29, 31, 32, 35, 42, 43; Courtesy NASA, Visible Earth Collection: pages 4, 22; Courtesy National Archives and Records Administration: pages 40, 41; Courtesy National Library of Canada: pages 12, 14, 23; Courtesy National Oceanic and Atmospheric Administration: Title Page, pages 5, 11, 24, 38, 39; © Susan Daniels: page 38; Courtesy www.pdphoto. com: page 9; Courtesy Rohm Padilla: page13; Courtesy U.S. Fish and Wildlife Service: page 15.

Edited by Jill Sherman

Cover design by Nicola Stratford, bdpublishing.com

Interior layout by Tara Raymo

Library of Congress PCN Data

Thompson, Linda
 Exploring The Great Lakes / Linda Thompson.
 ISBN 978-1-62169-835-7 (hard cover)
 ISBN 978-1-62169-7305 (soft cover)
 ISBN 978-1-62169-9392 (e-Book)
 Library of Congress Control Number: 2013936384

Also Available as:

Rourke Educational Media
Printed in the United States of America,
North Mankato, Minnesota

Rourke

rourkeeducationalmedia.com
customerservice@rourkeeducationalmedia.com • PO Box 643328 Vero Beach, Florida 32964

Table of Contents

Chapter 1
Waterway to America's Heartland

Several years after Christopher Columbus sailed to the New World in 1492 and 1493, a few other Europeans began coming to America for seasonal work. They were sailors from the coast of France who spent summers fishing the shoals of Newfoundland. Here, the cold ocean waters teemed with cod, a type of fish up to 6 feet (1.8 meters) long and weighing as much as 200 pounds (91 kilograms). Cod could be preserved with salt after it was caught and then dried or pickled and sold when the men returned to France.

Newfoundland was settled by fishermen in the early 1500s.

QUEBEC

Jacques Cartier Passage

NEWFOUNDLAND

Gulf of
St. Lawrence

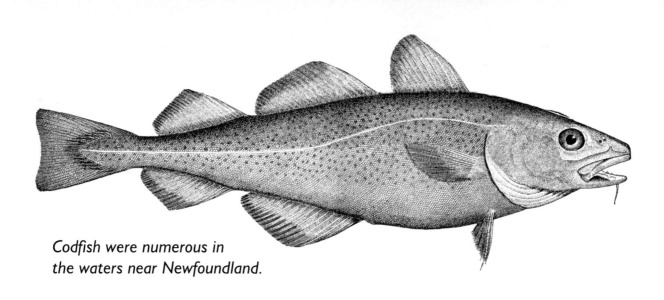

Codfish were numerous in the waters near Newfoundland.

A good summer's catch could support a fisherman and his family for the rest of the year. Soon, Basque, English, and Portuguese fishing boats could also be seen on the Newfoundland coast.

The shoals of Newfoundland had so many codfish that a fisherman could just scoop them right out of the water with a bucket.

Vikings came on ships to North America in search of supplies like timber.

From northwest France, the shores of North America are only about 2,500 miles (4,023 kilometers) away. Columbus traveled almost twice that far, more than 4,500 miles (7,242 kilometers) to get from Spain to the Bahamas, where he first landed. So it is not surprising that northern Europeans such as the French found it easier to explore the shores of what is now Canada. In fact, 500 years before Columbus's voyages, Scandinavians known as Vikings had also visited the North American coast and even tried unsuccessfully to settle there.

French fishermen generally did not keep ship logs, but their reports of the new land quickly reached the ears of their king, François I. Increasingly worried about Spain's growing power in the Americas, he sent an Italian explorer, Giovanni da Verrazzano, across the sea in 1523. Verrazzano's mission was to establish a claim to North American lands and also look for a water route to the Far East. Europeans were always seeking more direct ways to reach China, India, and present-day Indonesia, where they could buy valuable trade goods such as silk and spices.

Verrazzano's voyage launched a short but remarkable period of harmony and cooperation between Europeans and **indigenous peoples** that was very different from the conflicts **colonists** brought to other parts of the New World. The success of New France depended on water-based travel. At one time New France included the mighty Mississippi River and five immense lakes,

Giovanni da Verrazzano (1485–1528)

Giovanni da Verrazzano's mission was to navigate the shores between Florida and Newfoundland for a passage to the Pacific Ocean.

which hold one-fifth of all of the fresh surface water on Earth! Today these lakes, Lake Superior, Lake Michigan, Lake Huron, Lake Erie, and Lake Ontario, are known as the Great Lakes of the United States and Canada.

Verrazzano, however, never saw the Great Lakes or the Mississippi. He reached the Atlantic coast somewhere near present-day North Carolina and sailed to Cape Breton Island, northwest of Nova Scotia, before turning for home. Perhaps because of the region's heavy fogs, he missed the doorway to a part of America that would later be fiercely fought over by Britain and France. This doorway was the Gulf of St. Lawrence located on the eastern coast of what is now Canada.

It was up to another explorer, Jacques Cartier, to find this opening into the North American continent and its riches of fish, fur, timber, and minerals. In 1534, Cartier left France in two small ships. He was also searching for the waterway to the East and must have thought he had found it when he sailed into the Gulf of St. Lawrence. He explored its shoreline, installed a large cross to claim the region for François I, and sailed home. Returning in 1535 with three ships and a hundred men, he moved up the Fleuve St.-Laurent, or St. Lawrence River. The river led to a magnificent system of waterways that would prove extremely important to American trade and industry, but as Cartier probably realized, it did not lead to the Far East.

Jacques Cartier formed relations with the Iroquois to help him locate riches like silver, gold, and diamonds to bring back to France.

Not all of the glaciers in Canada melted. There are still many glaciers that can be visited.

ORIGIN OF THE GREAT LAKES

The five Great Lakes exist because of ice. More than a million years ago, enormous **glaciers** covered the land. They were as thick as 6,500 feet (2,000 meters). Their weight depressed the soil where rivers had existed before the glaciers crept southward from the North Pole. About 12,000 years ago, as the Earth's climate warmed, the glaciers retreated toward the north. Large amounts of melted water from the glaciers collected in the depressions, forming the five Great Lakes and the many rivers that connect to them.

Upon Jacques Cartier's arrival in Hochelaga, over a thousand people came to greet him. Now a bridge at that spot stands in his name.

Cartier landed at a **First Nations** village called Stadacona and decided to spend the winter there. This would become the site of Quebec, the oldest city in Canada. He also explored further upriver and exchanged gifts with indigenous peoples at the site of the present-day city of Montreal. The indigenous people described to Cartier an immense world of water, the Great Lakes, further to the west.

A FEW GREAT LAKES FACTS

The total amount of water in the five Great Lakes is about six quadrillion gallons (22,710,000,000,000 kiloliters). If it were spread evenly across the lower 48 states, this water would stand about 9.5 feet (2.9 meters) deep. The Great Lakes cover more than 94,000 square miles (243,460 square kilometers), and drain an area twice that size. Lake Superior contains 10 percent of the Earth's fresh water and by surface area is the largest freshwater lake in the world (31,700 square miles or 82,100 square kilometers). Including the islands they contain, the Great Lakes have more than 10,000 miles (16,090 kilometers) of coastline. Canada and the United States share four of the lakes, with only Lake Michigan lying entirely within the United States.

The French explorer Jean Nicolet was the first European to discover Lake Michigan in the 1630s.

Chapter 2
Champlain's Explorations

Samuel de Champlain (1574-1635)

Cartier and others made a few more voyages to North America, but it was not until 70 years later, in 1604, that Samuel de Champlain confirmed French claims to the region. He was a geographer sent by a religious leader, Pierre du Gua, Sieur de Monts, to found a permanent colony for the Huguenots. Champlain would later be called the father of New France.

Champlain wrote an account in 1632 of his three decade tour of North America that included a map of the region.

LES
VOYAGES
DE LA
NOVVELLE FRANCE
OCCIDENTALE, DICTE
CANADA,
FAITS PAR LE S*R DE CHAMPLAIN
Xainctongeois, Capitaine pour le Roy en la Marine du
Ponant, & toutes les Descouvertes qu'il a faites en

The Huguenots were a **sect** of the Protestant church seeking religious freedom in the New World. Champlain chose a site for them in present-day Nova Scotia, which they called Acadia. Three years later he founded the settlement of Quebec next to Stadacona. From 1609 to 1615, Champlain traveled on the St. Lawrence River and connecting waterways to what is now Lake Champlain in New York. He also explored westward to Lake Ontario and Lake Huron.

A map of Champlain's first voyage through North America.

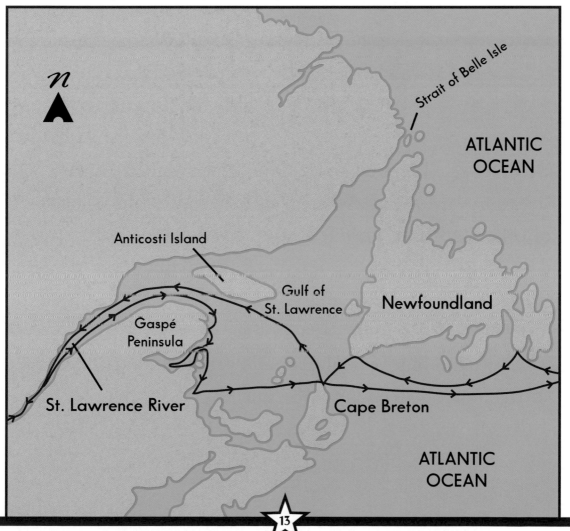

Natives of Canada taught Europeans how to make maple sugar.

At that time, about 120 **bands** of indigenous peoples lived in the Great Lakes region. In Canada, Native American tribes are called First Nations. Champlain was impressed to find people living comfortably in the cold, harsh environment, meeting all of their needs for food, shelter, and survival. Bands often traveled hundreds of miles by canoe down the Ottawa and St. Lawrence rivers to a trading center called Three Rivers, now Montreal, where they exchanged animal pelts for other goods they needed. Some bands in the northern parts of this region brought wild rice or maple sugar. They gathered the sugar from maple trees in early spring. Other popular trading centers were near the sites of present-day Chicago, Illinois; Sault Sainte Marie and Mackinaw, Michigan; and Green Bay, Wisconsin.

Places like Agassiz National Wildlife Refuge in Minnesota around the Great Lake area include many different types of lands including marshes and woodlands.

FORESTS AND BOGS

The Great Lakes region was a paradise for animals and plants, hunters, and fishermen. The southern areas supported vast stands of oak, maple, and other hardwood trees, with prairies where grass grew as high as 10 feet (3 meters). In the north, evergreen trees such as pine and fir grew in the shallow, sandy soils with many miles of bogs and marshes near water. In the forests and grasslands lived a large variety of wildlife including moose, deer, bear, wolves, foxes, mink, and other fur-bearing species. Thousands of species of birds thrived there, and about 180 kinds of fish lived in the lakes and rivers.

The First Nations in this area belong to a larger group that **anthropologists** call Northeast Woodlands people. They depended to a large degree on forest products for their survival. Great Lakes bands hunted, fished, gathered wild foods, and grew crops such as corn and tobacco. Like other indigenous peoples in the sixteenth century, they were very interested in European tools and objects such as needles, fishhooks, hatchets, traps, cooking pots, fabric, beads, knives, and guns. They began trading furs and skins for these things. European traders badly wanted the animal pelts, especially beavers, because beaver hats were popular in Europe. This made the beaver a valuable creature. In the Northeast Woodlands where fur-bearing animals were plentiful, the economy revolved around this industry. The fur trade shaped the history of the Great Lakes region, which soon involved bloody wars between France and England and their First Nations **allies**.

From the start, the French had developed an alliance with Algonkian-speaking tribes and the Iroquoian-speaking Huron group. In New York, Dutch colonists formed similar alliances with the five Iroquois nations known as the League of the Iroquois. When the English conquered New Netherland in 1664 and renamed it New York, those Iroquois groups transferred their loyalties to the English.

SOME GREAT LAKES TRIBES

The Great Lakes have played a vital role in the lives of indigenous peoples, who have lived along their shores for centuries. Most of those groups, such as the Menominee, Ottawa, Sauk, Fox, Potawatomi, and Ojibwe or Chippewa spoke languages in the Algonkian language family. The Oneida, Erie, and Huron were Iroquoian-speaking groups. The Winnebago or Ho-chunk, who speak Siouan, still live in Wisconsin.

Groups from other areas moved into the Great Lakes area under pressure from the Iroquois League to the east. These groups included the Miami, Mascouten, and Kickapoo.

The Chippewa built birchbark canoes for fishing and navigating through the Great Lakes.

Many other French explorers, traders, and missionaries would follow Champlain into the Great Lakes region. Some of the seventeenth-century explorers were Étienne Brulé, Jean Nicolet, Pierre Radisson, and the Sieur des Groseilliers. Within a few years, these adventurers had explored, traded, and developed alliances with the indigenous peoples in the woodlands throughout the Great Lakes region. The indigenous peoples taught the French survival and boating techniques, skills they needed in this often hostile environment. By the middle of the century, France had claimed the entire network of waterways from the St. Lawrence River through the Great Lakes and down the Mississippi Valley to the Gulf of Mexico.

THE IROQUOIS LEAGUE

In the mid-1550s, five Iroquoian-speaking tribes formed an alliance called the Iroquois League. The five tribes were the Mohawk, Seneca, Cayuga, Onandaga, and Oneida. Much later in 1772, the Tuscarora joined the league. This alliance was well organized and had a written constitution that may have influenced the development of the U.S. Constitution.

The eventual effect of the fur trade on **Native Americans** was that many bands abandoned their traditional ways of making a living and became dependent on European tools and trade. They were also drawn into the political plots of their European allies. The Iroquois had always been more warlike than the Algonkian groups, and first the Dutch, then the British, took advantage of this trait to attempt to weaken French economic and political power in the region.

The Winnebago had once called the European's guns thunderbirds thinking the guns were holy. They soon learned to use guns and traded furs for guns.

Chapter 3

Forts, Missions, and Trading Posts

Jacques Marquette (1637-1675)

Christian missionaries, especially members of the Society of Jesus, or Jesuits, accompanied some of the early French explorers. This Roman Catholic order first arrived to **convert** the Huron people in 1625. The Jesuits had strict standards for new converts so unlike other missionaries in America, they did not persuade large numbers of natives to become Christians. Nevertheless, between 1671 and 1701 the French established a chain of small missions at strategic points around the five lakes and at the gateway to the Mississippi. One of the best known of the Jesuits was Father Jacques Marquette, who accompanied Louis Joliet down the Mississippi in 1673. They are said to have been the first Europeans on the upper Mississippi River.

Each Jesuit mission usually included a trading post where *coureurs de bois* or runners of the woods gathered. These bold adventurers lived in the forest, often took indigenous peoples' women as wives, and trapped and traded with local tribes. Military troops sometimes used the trading posts, but they were not built primarily for defense. Each fort had a small permanent population, which included an administrator, a few farming families, a mission, a trading post, and often a nearby Native American village. This population expanded from time to time as traders, soldiers, and missionaries who were passing through paused to rest and restock supplies.

Lake Superior was often used in the fur trade, which began in 1658 by the French explorers Pierre-Esprit Radisson and Médard des Groseilliers.

Some of the early forts were Sault Sainte Marie between Lake Superior and Lake Huron; St. Ignace Mission on Mackinac Island between Lake Huron and Lake Michigan; Fort St. Croix near the western **portage** to Lake Superior; and La Baye at the southern tip of Green Bay on Lake Michigan. In 1701, a French nobleman, Antoine de la Mothe Cadillac built Fort Pontchartrain on Lake St. Clair, a small lake between Lake Huron and Lake Erie. This settlement would become the city of Detroit, Michigan.

Some early forts around the Great Lakes that were involved in trade.

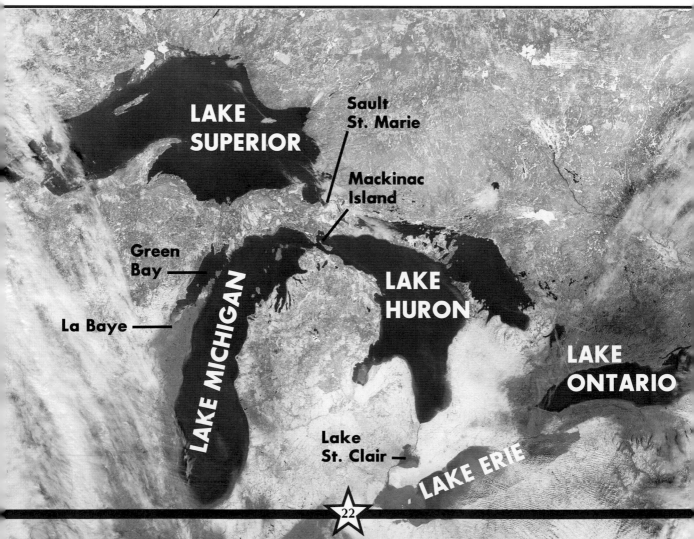

GREEN BAY

La Baye, which became Green Bay, Wisconsin, is the oldest settlement in Wisconsin. Champlain's lieutenant, Jean Nicolet, founded it near a Winnebago village at the mouth of the Fox River in 1634. In 1669, a Jesuit missionary, Claude Allouez, built a mission there. La Baye became an important rendezvous for traders, trappers, soldiers, and settlers through the eighteenth century. After the British conquered New France, they renamed the town Green Bay.

As the French extended their trading network, wars broke out between the Iroquois and the local tribes that assisted the French. During the French and Iroquois Wars of the mid 1600s, the Iroquois managed to largely destroy the power of the Huron, Erie, Conestoga, Illinois, and a number of other French allies. They also killed hundreds of French people, including many priests. In 1666, Jean Talon led an army of nearly a thousand French troops to a decisive victory over the Iroquois. That defeat brought relative peace for several decades.

The first Iroquois War was in 1609. The later wars were known as the French and Iroquois Wars or the Beaver Wars.

LA SALLE'S EXPLORATIONS

In 1668 explorer René Robert Cavelier, Sieur de la Salle, arrived in New France. He established Fort Frontenac on Lake Ontario and Fort Niagara above Niagara Falls. He is best known for traveling down the Mississippi River to its mouth in 1682 and claiming the entire region for his king, Louis XIV of France. From that voyage, the French were able to assert ownership of the huge region known as Louisiana.

This peaceful period encouraged the French to expand into the western section of the Great Lakes region. King Louis XIV sent more than 950 girls to marry French soldiers and settlers. They were nicknamed *les filles du Roi*, or the king's girls. In 1671, a delegate of the king held a ceremony at Sault Sainte-Marie with 14 local tribes attending, and claimed the entire western half of the continent for Louis XIV.

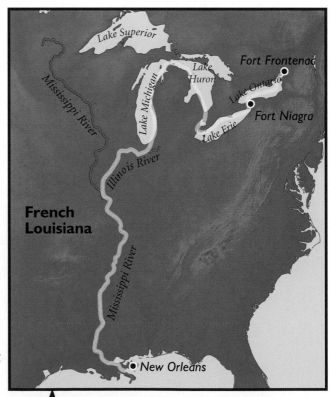

La Salle explored the Great Lakes and Mississippi River for France in 1862.

The Great Lakes and its rivers were the only practical means of moving people and freight during the colonial period. In summer, traders used 40-foot (12-meter) long birchbark canoes to bring goods such as woolen blankets, linen, copper kettles, steel knives, and beads to the trading posts. Then, using 25-foot (7.6-meter) long canoes, winter traders headed up rivers and streams to buy furs in Native American villages. La Salle was the first person to experiment with boats other than canoes. He built the *Frontenac*, a small barque that became Lake Ontario's first sailing ship and followed it with the *Griffon*, a 40-ton (36-metric ton) **schooner** with elegant carvings. To La Salle's dismay, in 1679 the *Griffon* and its load of furs disappeared on the way to Fort Niagara. Over more than three centuries, ships and boats have played a major role in the region's history. Hundreds of them sank with their cargoes because of storms, fires, collisions, and underwater hazards.

La Salle originally built the Griffon *schooner to find a passage to the Pacific Ocean.*

Two forts, Pontchartrain and St. Joseph, protected the water route through Lake Ontario and Lake Erie, allowing French trading to reach southward into present-day Illinois, Indiana, and Ohio. Other forts, built from 1683 to 1703 in the river valleys to the southwest, extended French influence into Illinois country. In these fertile valleys, French settlers grew corn and other food to supply missions and trading posts to the north.

Between 1750 and 1755, New France built or rebuilt about a dozen new forts. Meanwhile, English traders and settlers were flowing into the Ohio Valley. The last two forts, Fort Le Boeuf and Fort Duquesne, the future site of Pittsburgh, Pennsylvania, finally provoked the British. The resulting confrontation was a turning point that helped decide the fate of the Great Lakes region.

The Mi'kmaq in Miramichi, a French settlement on the Gulf of St. Lawrence, battled the British forces that arrived on their land in 1779.

Chapter 4
Conflict Between the French and British

Between 1689 and 1763, the French and British fought four wars that were at least partially about ownership of North America. After King William's War (1689-1697), Queen Anne's War (1702-1713), and King George's War (1744-1748), France lost some of its power. It was also forced to give up a large amount of land in 1713, including Acadia, Newfoundland, and Hudson's Bay.

The fourth conflict, the French and Indian War, was the final blow for France. It lasted from 1754 until 1763 and grew into a larger conflict called the Seven Years' War between France, England, and other European countries. A small contingent of troops from the newly constructed Fort Le Boeuf seized an English trading post. The English governor of Virginia sent a 22-year-old lieutenant colonel named George Washington to western Pennsylvania to protest. But his 150 troops were defeated and he returned home.

George Washington, (1732–1799), advanced quickly through the ranks of the army and became a senior officer during the first part of the French and Indian War.

The British took over Fort Niagara in July of 1759 during the Battle of Fort Niagara.

In March of 1754 Washington returned with 300 Virginia **militia** to build a fort at the forks of the Ohio River. In July, more than 600 French and Native American troops attacked it. Washington surrendered and was released again. The following year, the French had another victory at Fort Niagara, routing a British force attempting to take Fort Duquesne. In 1756 the war spread to Europe. In America, French troops successfully captured a number of English posts. But in 1758 the tide turned.

The British commanded Fort Niagara throughout the Revolutionary War.

In all of French Canada there were only about 60,000 people, compared with nearly 1 million in the English colonies. A new British prime minister, William Pitt, believed that unless the Canadians received heavy reinforcements from France, they could not hold out against naval attacks. The British took Quebec in 1759, and in the spring of 1760 they surrounded Montreal. In September of that year the Governor of Canada surrendered his country to England.

NAMING CANADA

In 1535 Jacques Cartier asked two First Nations youths the way to Stadacona and heard the word "Kanata," which meant village or settlement in the Huron-Iroquois dialect. Cartier used Canada to refer to the entire undefined region. In 1547 everything north of the St. Lawrence River was designated on French maps as Canada. The St. Lawrence River was called the Riviere de Canada until the early 1600s.

During this war the Iroquois had sided with the British, while the Menominee, Ho-chunk, Ojibwa, and Potawatomi were allied with the French. When the war ended, the British had won all of the French possessions in Canada and the Midwest. The Peace of Paris in 1763 also gave England control of the St. Lawrence, the door to the Great Lakes. In a secret treaty the year before, France had given the huge territory of Louisiana to Spain. After 1763, France was left with only a few islands off Newfoundland and in the West Indies.

THE FRENCH INFLUENCE REMAINS

Cajun people have established a rich culture including food and music in Louisiana.

Nearly 250 years after the fall of Montreal, French is still the main language of the Canadian province of Quebec. The Acadians, banished by the British from Nova Scotia in 1755, scattered from Maine to Georgia, with many settling around New Orleans. French is still spoken there, and Cajun traditions remain strong. French names throughout the Great Lakes region are a reminder of the colonial heyday of the French in America.

The British controlled Quebec for over 100 years after taking it over in 1760.

When France lost its American territory, the era of friendly **coexistence** between Europeans and indigenous people came to a close. The British treated the indigenous people formerly allied with the French like conquered people. For example, they ended the French practice of giving supplies, ammunition, and payments to indigenous leaders to ensure their cooperation. They stopped supplying rum, which many indigenous people had become dependent upon. Instead of seeing themselves as respected partners of the Europeans, indigenous people began to feel exploited. One result was Pontiac's Rebellion in the Ohio Valley in 1763.

Chief **Pontiac** of the Ottawa people led the tribes against the British. He hoped to drive them out of the Great Lakes region and return control to the French. Pontiac's forces attacked and captured many British forts, including those at the Straits of Mackinac, but they failed to take Montreal or Detroit. But after the French and Canadians refused to join his rebellion, it lost its intensity. By 1765 the British had managed to regain control of the region.

Chief Pontiac decided to take revenge on the British because he wanted better treatment for First Nations.

Chief Pontiac and three hundred of his armed men fought to take over Old Fort Detroit in 1763 for many months until Pontiac finally gave up.

THE FOUNDING OF DETROIT

Antoine Laumet de la Mothe Cadillac, a French military leader and trader, was in charge of Fort Michilimackinac on the Strait of Mackinac, now in Michigan, from 1694 to 1697. In 1698, Cadillac asked King Louis XIV to let him establish a French outpost along le detroit, a waterway connecting Lakes Erie and Huron. In 1763, Fort Detroit was one of few posts that withstood a months-long siege by Chief Pontiac's forces. Detroit was a strategic British military post during the American Revolutionary War (1775-1783). But after the war ended, the British refused to give up Detroit and other western outposts. On July 11, 1796, U.S. soldiers took Detroit from the British, and the Michigan Territory became part of the United States.

Chapter 5
The Northwest Territory

Pontiac's Rebellion taught the British that success in the Great Lakes region depended on having good relations with Native Americans. This policy paid off when the American Revolution began in 1775, and almost all Great Lakes peoples sided with the British. America gained its independence when the British surrendered in 1781, and another Treaty of Paris was signed on September 3, 1783. During these negotiations, the current international boundary bisecting the Great Lakes was set. However, fearing that the new United States would take away their lands, many Great Lakes tribes continued to support the British.

The **Northwest Ordinance** of 1787, written for the **Northwest Territory**, was later applied to other land acquisitions. It stated that a territory would go from a colony with an appointed governor to self-government with an elected assembly and finally to statehood. The act provided for democratic rights, public education, and freedom of religion. The act did not allow slavery in new territories. This was a progressive piece of legislation that set an orderly course for national expansion.

However, strong alliances between the British and the Native Americans obstructed American expansion. From the beginning, Native Americans were not considered citizens of the United States because tribes had **sovereignty**. Therefore, it was difficult for the U.S. government to demand their loyalty. Britain still held Fort Niagara and other posts on the Great Lakes and continued to engage in the fur trade throughout the region.

A map of the Northwest Territory, 1787.

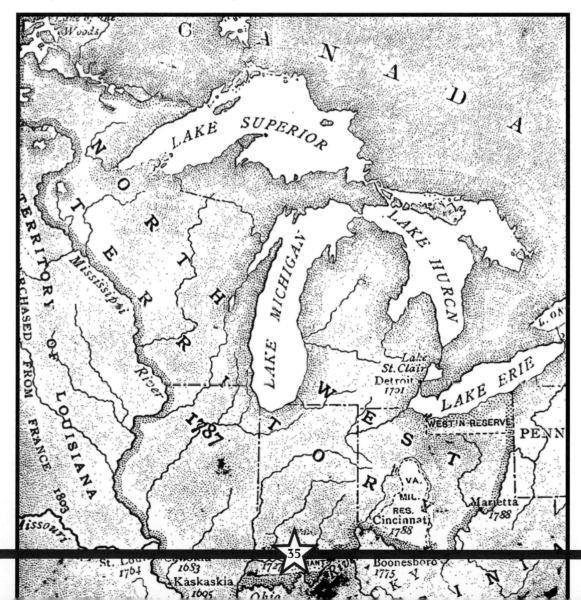

In 1791, 2,000 troops led by General Arthur St. Clair, governor of the Northwest Territory, tried to build a fort at the present site of Fort Wayne, Indiana. Native American tribes carried out a surprise attack and killed more than 900 men. The United States tried to persuade Britain to give up trading posts in the Northwest Territory, but Britain refused. Finally, in 1794, Major General Anthony Wayne led several thousand troops up the Maumee River. Nearly 2,000 Miami, Shawnee, Ottawa, Chippewa, Potawotomi, Sauk, and Fox, along with 70 Canadian rangers, faced Wayne's forces at the Battle of Fallen Timbers. The place was named for a stockade of felled trees south of present-day Toledo, Ohio behind which the tribes made their stand.

Wayne's forces were victorious and went on to destroy Native American villages and crops. In the Treaty of Greenville of 1795, Native Americans gave up huge areas of land in the southeastern Great Lakes region. This treaty opened up the Northwest Territory for U.S. settlement. Subsequent treaties with Native Americans in 1807 and 1819 saw most of the remaining tribes either confined to small reservations or pushed out of the region altogether.

In the Battle of Fallen Timbers, the fallen tree served as a sort of obstacle course that the Native Americans expertly navigated and hid behind.

MINERAL RICHES

On the shores of Lake Superior, First Nations mined copper for centuries before French explorers arrived. Other minerals that occur in significant amounts in the region are lead and iron. However, First Nations claims to minerals were lost when the Chippewa and the Sioux made peace with the United States and established a boundary line in the Treaty of

Prairie du Chien in 1826. One clause of the treaty said, "The Chippewa tribe grants to the government of the United States the right to search for, and carry away, any metals or minerals from any part of their country."

Minerals like iron would support the Great Lakes economy for many years to come.

Today, boats are still the best way to transport heavy cargo.

The United States would engage Britain once more in the War of 1812. England had been losing sailors to American ships. British ships began to stop American ships and **impress** any British-born crew, forcing them back onto British ships. The U.S. also wanted to stop Native American populations from supporting the British because it was impeding American expansion. President Thomas Jefferson had acquired the immense Louisiana Territory from France in 1803 and wanted to make it safe for new settlers.

THE BEGINNINGS OF CHICAGO

One area the U.S. government received in the Treaty of Greenville was a swampy piece of land on Lake Michigan near a river that Native Americans called Checagou. In 1803, the army built Fort Dearborn on this site. About 100 people lived in the area until the War of 1812,

when 400 Potawatomi warriors, agents of the British, massacred some of the inhabitants and burned the fort. Some years later, the city of Chicago arose on the site and was incorporated in 1837.

Today, Chicago is the third largest city in the United States.

In the Battle of Lake Erie, the U.S. took the lake with their nine ships that defeated the British's six ships.

The war was fought on land, mostly around the Great Lakes region, and at sea. England was the stronger force until 1814, when the tables turned. Several decisive battles put the British on the defensive, and the Battle of Lake Erie was a turning point. However, several months later British troops marched to the U.S. capital, Washington, D.C., and burned many public buildings. The war ended in favor of the United States when troops led by General Andrew Jackson won a number of battles in the southern states.

On January 8, 1815, Jackson defeated the British navy, including more than 2,000 men, at the Battle of New Orleans. This victory gave Americans much needed national pride, even though a peace treaty, the Treaty of Ghent, had already been signed by negotiators in Belgium on December 24, 1814.

The Erie Canal connected Lake Erie to the Hudson River and took seventeen years to build.

New York State's completion of the Erie Canal in 1825 triggered a development boom in the Great Lakes region. Shipping costs plunged, and it became much easier for settlers to travel from New York City inland to Cleveland or Detroit. When railroads were built from Chicago to the Mississippi River in the 1850s, that city surpassed Detroit as a magnet for immigrants and industry.

As westbound settlers filled the Great Lakes region in the second half of the nineteenth century, massive changes occurred. The new residents cut the forests, overfished the waterways, and plowed the land for farming. The wastes from timber cutting clogged streams and rivers. As the population grew, wildlife numbers sharply declined. The development of industry caused chemical pollution of lakes and rivers. During the last half of the twentieth century, the U.S. passed laws to regulate pollution. Gradually, the forests, fish habitat, and soil of the region have begun to make a recovery.

Biographies

Many people played important roles throughout this time period. Learn more about them in the Biographies section.

Columbus, Christopher (1451-1506) - Italian explorer in the service of Spain who discovered America for the Europeans in 1492.

Cartier, Jacques (1491-1557) - French explorer sent by François I to find a northwest passage to the Far East.

François I (1494-1547) - King of France 1515-1547.

Monts, Pierre du Gua, Sieur de (1560-1630) - French Huguenot explorer and colonizer in North America.

Champlain, Samuel de (1567-1635) - French explorer and founder of New France.

Brulé, Étienne (1591-1633) - French explorer who came to Quebec in 1608 with Samuel de Champlain.

Nicolet, Jean (1598-1642) - French explorer in North America; the first European to explore the western Great Lakes.

Groseilliers, Sieur des, Médard Chouart (1618 - 1710) - A *coureur de bois*, one of the first Europeans to penetrate deep into the forests of the Great Lakes region.

Allouez, Claude (1622-1689) - Early French missionary in Canada.

Talon, Jean (1625-1694) - French colonial leader in Canada, 1665-1668 and 1670-1672.

Radisson, Pierre (1636-1710) - Brother-in-law of the Sieur des Groseilliers, helped explore the upper reaches of the Mississippi and Missouri rivers.

Marquette, Jacques (1637-1675) - French Jesuit missionary and explorer in America.

Louis XIV (1638-1715) - King of France 1643-1715, known as the Sun King.

La Salle, René Robert Cavelier, Sieur de (1643-1687) - French explorer in North America. Explored the Mississippi to its mouth and claimed the land for Louis XIV of France (1682).

Joliet, Louis (1646-1700) - French-Canadian explorer, one of first on the upper Mississippi River.

Cadillac, Antoine de la Mothe (1658-1730) - French colonial administrator who founded Detroit in 1701.

Pontiac, Chief (1720–1769) - Leader of the Chippewa, Potawatomi, and Ottawa tribes.

St. Clair, Arthur (1736-1818) - Governor of the Northwest Territory 1787-1802.

Jackson, Andrew (1767-1845) - Seventh President of the United States (1829-1837).

Timeline

CE 1000
Leif Eriksson, a Viking, sails to the coast of what is probably Newfoundland.

1492
Christopher Columbus lands on an island in what is now the Bahamas, opening the door to European immigration to America.

1523-1524
Giovanni da Verrazano explores the coastline of present-day Canada, establishing a French claim to North America.

1534-1535
Jacques Cartier explores the Gulf of St. Lawrence and the St. Lawrence River.

1604-1608
Champlain arrives in the New World, founds Acadia for the Huguenots, and establishes a trading post at Quebec.

1625
Jesuit priests arrive in New France to convert the Huron people.

1642-1653
Iroquois War, in which the Iroquois wipe out Native American allies of France.

1666
Jean Talon leads French troops to victory over the Iroquois.

1673
Father Jacques Marquette and Louis Joliet explore the upper Mississippi River.

1682
La Salle claims the entire Mississippi River watershed for France.

1683-1755
The French build a chain of forts reaching to the Mississippi.

1701
Cadillac builds Fort Pontchartrain, later Detroit.

1713
Queen Anne's War, after which the French lose Acadia, Newfoundland, and Hudson's Bay to Britain.

1754-1763
The French and Indian War, resulting in France losing all American possessions except for a few islands to Britain.

1776-1783
The American Revolution.

1791-1794
Series of skirmishes between British-allied Native American groups and U.S. settlers and troops, ending with U.S. victory in the Battle of Fallen Timbers.

1795
Treaty of Greenville opens up formerly Native American lands for American settlement.

1812-1814
The War of 1812, ending with the Treaty of Ghent on December 24, 1814.

Reference

Map of the Great Lakes

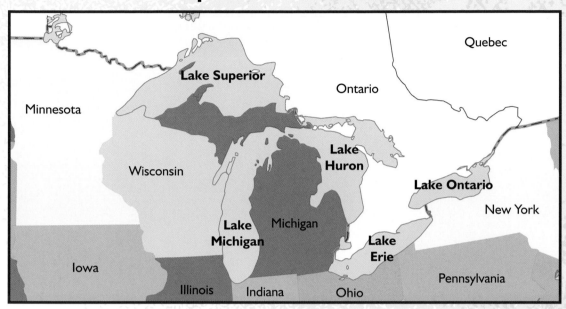

Map of Territories of Native American Peoples

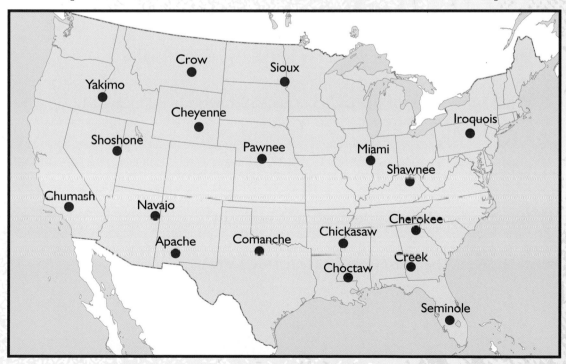

● Native American Territories

Websites to Visit

www.kidskonnect.com/subjectindex/28-places/geography.html

www.epa.gov/glnpo/atlas/glat-ch1.html

www.great-lakes.net/teach/history/native/native_1.html

Show What You Know

1. How many gallons of water are in the five Great Lakes?

2. What were some of the indigenous tribes who lived along the Great Lakes?

3. When did Champlain arrive in the New World?

4. What is the oldest settlement in Wisconsin?

5. What were the five Great Lakes formed by?

Glossary

allies (AL-eyez): people or countries that are on the same side during a war or conflict

anthropologist (an-thruh-PAH-luh-jist): person who studies human beings

bands (bands): groups of native people who stay together out of a common purpose

coexistence (koh-ig-ZIST-uhns): living in peace with each other as a matter of policy

colonist (KAH-luh-nist): people who establish a colony or settle a new land or region

convert (KAHN-vurt): to convince a person to change beliefs; a person who has changed from one belief to another

First Nations (furst NAY-shuhns): what Native American tribes are called in Canada

glaciers (GLAY-shurz): bodies of ice moving down a valle or spreading out on a land surface

impress (im-PRES): forcing one into service, especially naval service

militia (muh-LISH-uh): body of citizens organized for military service

Native Americans (NAY-tiv uh-MER-i-kuhns): one of the peoples who originally lived in North, Central, or South America or descendents of these people

Northwest Ordinance (NORTH-west OR-duh-nuhns): U.S. law of 1787 that described when settled land could become a territory or a state and defined the rights of people living there

Northwest Territory (NORTH-west TER-i-tor-ee): also known as the "Old Northwest," the region north of the Ohio River, east of the Mississippi, and including the southern and western shores of the Great Lakes

portage (POR-tij): route followed in carrying boats or goods overland from one body of water to another or around an obstacle such as a rapids

schooner (SKOO-nur): sailing ship with two masts

sect (sekt): group, usually religous, with a specific doctrine and a leader

sovereignty (SAHV-ruhn-tee): independent power or freedom from outside control

Index